Green Your Heart

Green Your World

Avoid Burnout, Save the World, & Love Your Life

Elizabeth B. Hill, MSW

ISBN: 9780999197608

DEDICATION

For Raven & James

CONTENTS

ACKNOWLEDGMENTS

To the many dear ones that have shaped the pages of this book and the chapters of my life, I give thanks.

Many people contributed to this book by providing feedback, edits and advice, including Colleen Brunetti, Jenn Cavalleri, Cheryl Hale, Liz Lockwood, Nancy Micloskey, Donna Osuch, Meghan Sharron, Ali Shepherd, and all my friends and teammates at Accomplishment Coaching. Emily Juricek, my life coach, deserves my immense gratitude for her unwavering support and always keeping me focused on the bigger picture. Thank you to my yoga students who have helped create the many practices in this book.

Thank you to my friends and colleagues at United Way of West Central CT for their laughter, kindness, and support. Thank you to the many community rockstars I know and work with, including my dear friend Pat Stebbins, who inspire me to keep making a difference.

Thank you to my mother, who taught me to believe in fairies, appreciate plate tectonics and made sure I knew I was loved every day of my life. Thank you to my father, the legendary Papa Steve, who always encouraged me to drive fast, take chances and dream big.

Thank you to my Aunt Ginny, Auntie Bert and Uncle Rick for their encouragement, laughter and wisdom. Thank you to my Grandma Betty Meyer for a lifetime of passionate, intelligent conversations and to my Grandma Betty Hill for inspiring me to never stop dancing or shaking things up. Thank you to my brother Chris for a lifetime of epic songs, adventures and love. Thank you to my children Raven and James for being such wonderful humans, in addition to the light of my life.

I would especially like to thank Michael Eck. He continues to say "Yes, And…!" to all my crazy dreams and is the embodiment of love in a human. I am very grateful to be on this wild adventure with him.

Thank you to my friends Melissa Faye Nocera, Anne Collin, Jim and Jaime Williams, Karla Archambeault, and Joe DiMaggio for witnessing all the variations of Liz and sticking around. They are my go-to team in times of crisis and I am eternally grateful for having them in my life.

Thank you to everyone who has helped make this book a reality and has helped make my life more beautiful, happier and filled with love.

INTRODUCTION

"Peace in ourselves, peace in our world." - Thich Nhat Hanh

"Tell me, what is it you plan to do with your one wild and precious life?"
- Mary Oliver

In truth, this book was written for me to learn, as I was writing.

Throughout my life, I have seen countless people run themselves into the ground in service of others. I hear of more and more people completely overwhelmed, taking on too much, having panic attacks and numbing out to deal with it all. These are often the people who spend their days working to make the world a better place.

One of my favorite quotes is from Fred Rogers, "When I was a boy and would see scary things on the news, my mother would say to me, 'Look for the helpers. You will always find people that are helping'."

I wrote this book to help these helpers: nonprofit professionals, teachers, parents, nurses, social workers, caregivers, community leaders, volunteers, and anyone else who spends their days in service to others. This book includes a wealth of soulful practices to help people avoid burnout, keep saving the world, and love their lives. I know the practices in this book work, because I have used them myself. I have taken my own turn saving the world at the expense of myself more times than I care to count.

Fifteen plus years ago, I was one scary, drunk, angry, anxious mess. On a mission to save the world, yes, but still one scary drunk, angry, anxious mess. Ten plus years ago I cleared out most of the scary and drunk, but continued as an anxious, depressed, shut-down mama. It has been a wild, uncomfortable, ugly journey, but I now have more joy, happiness, creativity, purpose, love, and laughter in my life than ever. I am clearly not perfect, but the days I am shut down or feel like a robot are much fewer and farther between. I am extremely grateful to report that I have found many healthy practices that work to make life better. These healthy practices have helped me as well as those around me, including my family, friends, and those I have spent my days helping in my professional capacities. I am on a mission to share these practices with as many people as possible.

We weren't made to go it alone, but somewhere along the line many of us got the message we needed to. Many of us were taught that independence and self-sufficiency are to be valued over love, compassion, health, and happiness. That doing for others was to be valued over empowering them. That our value was in saving and doing, rather than in being and sharing our gifts. I am here to tell you that you are enough.

In the words of Howard Thurman, "Don't ask what the world

needs. Ask what makes you come alive, and go do that. Because what the world needs is more people who have come alive."

I stumbled across these words at just the right time. Until that point, I had lived my life serving the world's needs all day. My "me-time" was allocated to a painfully small late night indulgence that generally included numbing out and shutting down. This cycle was, in biblical terms, hiding my light under a bushel. It had not occurred to me that by waking up and doing what I deeply loved, felt passionate about and was good at I could both serve the world and experience genuine happiness and fulfillment in the process. This was life changing.

In this book you will find meditations, restorative yoga poses, experiential and creative practices to try on today to help life feel lighter. You will find your way to living your life's purpose, sharing your own special light that you were created to share, and be empowered to be healthy, happy, and whole in the process.

Throughout the book, I use the term "greening". This is a word for transformation or growth. Greening is reflective of the process of growth and transformation present in nature. When I speak of greening your heart, I am referring to the process of returning to a balanced chakra system, with a heart and spirit that are thriving. The body contains seven chakras, or energy centers, through which energy flows. A chakra system that is out of balance can cause emotional, mental, and physical discomfort and illness.

Each chakra has a color associated with it. The color of the heart chakra, also called Anahata, is green. By greening our heart chakra, bringing our chakra system back into balance and learning to show love for ourselves in all our actions, we are greening our hearts and, by extension, our world.

As we deepen our connection with the natural world and live in alignment with our life's purpose, our body, and well-being thrive. This is the shift that greening our heart and all aspects of our life provide.

In this book, we will look at how greening in seven key areas can help you prevent burnout, save the world, and enjoy life in the process. These seven key areas are Filling Your Cup, Work, Home, Love, Money, Time and Community. We will explore how seeing the events of our life and the world around us through a lens of Gratitude, Abundance, and Compassion, can change our daily experience.

Throughout the book, you will find Green Heart Practices

designed to support greening in all of these key areas. Feel free to read through the book in order or skip around to try on practices as you feel drawn to them. Sometimes you may find you are connected with what you need just by turning a page at the right time. Enjoy!

WITH LOVE, LIZ

1 FILLING YOUR CUP

"Place the oxygen mask on yourself first before helping small children or others who may need your assistance." - Airplane Safety Instructions

"Rest and self-care are so important. When you take time to replenish your spirit, it allows you to serve others from the overflow. You cannot serve from an empty vessel." - Eleanor Brownn

When I first started practicing yoga, being still was pure torture. My body wanted to move-move-move. My mind was thinking – *'What's next? What have I forgotten? Who are these people around me? Am I doing this right?'* My brain also seemed to enjoy using this time to lay on a heavy layer of guilt. I would be on my mat seeking peace as my brain sifted through an endless stream of guilt over 500 past indiscretions, 498 of which were most definitely wildly unimportant.

Ashtanga/Power/Vinyasa yoga was the only way I could "do" yoga at that point. I could only welcome the final relaxation, savasana, after at least 60 minutes of constant movement. Each time the lights went down towards the end of class and the familiar mantra music switched on, I became a sobbing, weepy mess.

I've now taught yoga for 12 years and practiced for 18. It's been quite a trip. Restorative yoga and Yin, in which you hold poses for at least three to five minutes, are now my most favorite practices. It took me about six years of dedicated 'yoga-ing' to feel comfortable and actually enjoy relaxing for more than a minute.

Now, I can enjoy space between my thoughts instead of needing to fill up that space. I can rest for a moment without feeling crushing guilt. I can relax into poses, without bracing against some imagined, imminent doom. I couldn't have explained this feeling of rest before I experienced it myself.

A little bit ago, I found myself snowed under. I had gone through a divorce, was transitioning to a full-time job, was trying to figure out if I should move away or stay in the house I was in, while trying to juggle the blessings and responsibilities of kids and family. I stopped teaching classes and started "just" *taking* them.

It was in the midst of this hiatus that I went to a Restorative yoga class. In a supported child's pose, a thought moved through my body: "I deserve this". I had tried to instill this thought before, but it always felt false.

This was the very first time I truly believed it. In every cell of my body.

"I deserve this."

Let me be clear. I am blessed with work I love and I work hard at all of it. All the time. And I always have.

So why on earth has it taken me 38 years to believe that I

"deserve" to be still for 60 minutes?

I know for a certainty I am not alone in this. And this breaks my heart.

Many of us drive ourselves into the ground, perhaps believing that doing so provides a demonstration of our worth, proves our love to others, or we need to act this way in order to be loved. We may not realize there is any other way to be.

Why is this? What is this really about? Why do we believe worthiness is found through self-sacrifice? It sounds extreme, but I know I have spent 20 plus years in this space. Have you? Will you?

What if we were worth the space we take up? What if we were worth the time to honor, care, and nourish ourselves?

Let's honor ourselves enough to trust in our own worth and know this in every cell in our being.

One of the ways we can express this deep honoring of ourselves, is to take excellent care of ourselves and find practices that keep us happy, healthy and whole, that "fill our cup".

This is what I mean by the term "green your heart".

Green Your Heart

Greening our hearts means allowing for growth and seeking balance in our lives, our bodies, and our spirits. Through it we support the process of homeostasis present in nature by allowing for opportunities for movement, growth, and coming back to balance. Greening of our hearts means growth and taking care for ourselves. It also includes taking care of our loves, that which we hold close to our heart including our relationships, our people, and our passions.

In this book, we explore ways to take loving care of ourselves in all aspects: our health, our joys, our loves, our physical body, our finances, our home environments, our work environments, our relationships, and our communities.

Many of us were taught that loving ourselves was wrong. That there was something wrong with looking in the mirror and saying, "Damn, that is one fine looking lady!" or "Ooh, who's that handsome man looking back at me?" Some of us may have been taught that knowing what you are good at was the sin of pride, not confidence. That taking time on our appearance was vain, rather than letting our light shine.

When we place ourselves first through the lens of gratitude, compassion, and an abundant mindset, it is not a selfish action. It empowers us to 1) rock out our life purpose, and 2) take better care of our fellow humans, our families, our environment and our communities.

The key to greening our hearts is connecting with our love and passions and making sure those loves and passions are finding fulfillment in our relationships, our life's work, and daily life.

The following chapters share 32 Green Heart Practices that you can start putting into practice today to show love and care for yourself, make the world a better place, and add joy to your life and the lives of those around you.

On Wishing to Skip Over Ourselves

If you have picked up this book, chances are you are driven by a desire to skip over yourself. I have spent 12 years as a yoga instructor teaching people to stop, slow down and take a breath. Even for me, despite my training, it is still my go-to to want to speed things up and skip to the end.

I could agree in concept that everyone on earth deserves the space to pause, breathe and take care of themselves. However, when it came to my own life, I have viewed this as a luxury, an add-on, an item to add to the "if I could only find the time to…." list. From years of knowing mothers, social workers, community leaders, health care providers, and other caregiving professionals, this is all too common.

As Stephen R. Covey shares in his book "The 8th Habit: From Effectiveness to Greatness":

"You will clearly discover, if it's not already obvious to you, why there is no way you can make significant relationships with other people if your own life is a mess or if you're basically untrustworthy. That's why, in the last analysis, to improve any relationship, you must start with yourself."

For leaders and those that care for others, self-care is not a luxury. It is not a special present you give to yourself, nor is it something you feel you need to check off your to-do list or an extra burden. As a healer and helper in the world, you don't need another item on your to-do list.

Many of us have come to our work as a deep expression of love and care for others. And many of us carry with us, for some reason, a weight of guilt or burden. This may also be brought into our well-being. In redefining how to take care of ourselves, we also have the chance to shift what that means and remove any cloak of guilt or shame around it.

What message are we sending by not loving ourselves? As leaders, helpers, and caregivers, self-care is not just for our own well-being. It is a necessity so that we can care for others. In an airplane, in the event of an emergency, we are told the importance of putting our own oxygen mask on first, and then putting the mask on our children or others in need. This makes sense in that high crisis situation, but it is equally important in our day-to-day lives. We cannot be of service to others if we have passed out from lack of oxygen. We cannot be of service to others if we have driven ourselves into the ground.

Besides being a necessary element of self-care, valuing the importance of our well-being is also a leadership opportunity. By our caring for ourselves, we are giving others permission to do the same. (They don't need our permission, but they might think they do!) We are providing an example for our daughters, our sons, our volunteers, our staff, and everyone in our lives. We value the importance of caring for ourselves, not only for own happiness and well-being, but for the happiness and health of our children, our families, our communities, and our world.

Green Heart Practice:
Finding Your Way Back To You, Part 1
A Practice In Compassion

When people think of well-being they often think of going on a diet, stopping smoking, or getting a physical. While those may well end up on some people's well-being checklist, that is only a part of what we are searching for here. We are looking for what things will radically lighten your stress level, improve your quality of life, and make your days brighter. What brings you back to you? What makes you feel more alive and more like yourself, no matter what else is happening on that particular day in the world around you?

The world is full of the right ways to do things: the new fitness craze, the new vitamin supplement, the new stress-management technique. What will make you healthy, inside and out, is taking on a different practice for deep well-being which goes beyond the surface level of the things we think we "should" be doing. This involves having a deeper, clearer understanding of what you as an individual need to live a brighter, happier, more purposeful life. Finding the answer can take time, exploration, and self-inquiry. Dedicating space and time to exploring this is a beautiful expression of self-love, and a valuable component of building a life that maximizes the service and care we can provide for others.

To continue your exploration, reflect on the questions below to discover your own ways back to you.

Question 1: Imagine you had a day all to yourself. What would you be most excited to do? List four things you would love to incorporate into your day.

Question 2: What feels more nourishing and uplifting, a) a party, b) sharing a meal with one close friend, or c) time at home by yourself?

Question 3: Is there something regarding your health that you feel like you should be doing, but don't? Get clear on your commitments and the reasons why they are important to you.

Question 4: What is one thing that consistently gets in the way of your self-care? Examples include being late, always tired, an overbooked schedule, or lack of motivation.

Question 5: Answer the following phrase: I always feel better when I get to....

Take time to write a detailed response to each question. Once completed, use the guidelines in Part 2 to create a well-being plan for yourself.

"Learning to treat ourselves lovingly may at first feel like a dangerous experiment." - Sharon Salzberg

Finding Your Way Back To You, Part 2

We will now use your written responses from Part 1 to create a plan that will be supportive of your well-being.

Response to Question 1: Make your imaginary day real. You've listed four things you would love to do on your ideal day. Why wait? How could you weave more of these things into your life now? For instance, a 2-hour hike in the woods might be ideal but challenging to fit into every day. However, a 5-minute walk outside is more doable, as is adding an herb garden to your office. All provide a feeling of connection with nature.

Response to Question 2: Discover where you fall on the introversion/extroversion scale and create a schedule that supports your needs. This answer shows where you gain energy from and where you don't, pointing towards where you fall on the spectrum of introversion or extroversion. Discovering whether you need more time with people or alone to recharge is an important component of developing your own well-being plan.

For years, I thought I was an extrovert. I adored people, loved being on stage, and making people laugh. It wasn't until I had kids that I realized that throughout my life I'd craved alone time and preferred being one-on-one with people, rather than going to a party. Loving people and finding them fascinating didn't make me an extrovert.

Now, because I know I need alone time, both for working purposes and for relaxation, I add reading to my daily schedule and days that I work from home to my weekly schedule. These recharge me and give me a chance to refuel my energy and go out to do the work I love - helping others.

Response to Question 3: Get clear on your commitments and find your reason why. Take a few moments to get clear on what activities will actually support your well-being and your health. If you can't find a reason why, most likely you will not find yourself doing it. If it is worth doing being crystal clear on your motivation may support you in following through. If you are not able to find a clear reason, it might be worth letting go of.

Question 4: By finding out what gets in the way of self-care, you can create a plan to remove that obstacle. Lack of sleep has been an obstacle to my well-being for years. I would stay up well past midnight every night, wake up late and miserable, and always be late to work. I created a routine to get cozy in bed by 9:30 pm, reflect on the day from 9:30-10 pm, have wind-down time from 10-11 pm, with lights going out by 11. By doing this, I have been able to get the sleep I need, wake up at a good time and start work rested and significantly less frazzled. Whenever I fall out of the habit now, it feels off, and I actually desire to go back to the routine.

Question 5: Put yourself first. If something makes you feel better, then it should probably be done on the regular. And if YOU don't make it a priority, no one else will. Find a way to make these a priority and put them on your schedule first.

"Caring for myself is not self-indulgence. It is self-preservation."
- Audre Lorde

GREEN HEART PRACTICE:

WELL BEING TRACKER

A PRACTICE IN COMPASSION

In order to keep our integrity with our well-being, it is important to have some supports in place to make sure we fulfill our commitments. It would make sense that we would naturally do the things that feel good for our bodies and our well-being, but we often do not. It is so easy to let the busyness of the day, tugs of work, other people's needs, and our To-Do checklists overwhelm us. We need accountability structures to make sure we keep our integrity and commitments to ourselves.

One accountability structure is a well-being tracker. Choose up to 10 things you would like to incorporate into your daily schedule and start keeping track each day. You can write this down on paper, create an excel spreadsheet, make a list on whiteboard in your office, or use any other method you like.

To hold you accountable, find someone that you can share your results with on a weekly basis. You could share the whole sheet, or you could share the percentage you've completed. In my weekly session with my life coach, I report to my coach what percentage of my well-being list I have completed.

What continues to amaze me is that usually when I'm down about any aspect of my life at the end of the week (work, relationship, etc…) I look back and see that my well-being percentages are dreadfully low. On weeks when I've felt more powerful, more productive and more enthusiastic about life, my well-being list completion rate is high. There is a direct correlation. When I take care of myself in these areas, every other aspect of my life is better.

"If monks and nuns do not cherish their time of practice, they will have nothing to offer the world." - Thich Nhat Hanh

Green Heart Practice:

Metta Meditation

A Practice in Compassion

Metta meditation, also called "Loving Kindness meditation", is a beautiful, healing practice.

To begin, sit comfortably. Connect each of the following phrases with a deep breath in and a deep breath out. There is no need to speak the phrase aloud, unless you feel called to.

Read each phrase below and hold it in your mind and heart, connecting each phrase with the breath.

May I Be Safe

May I Be Happy

May I Be Healthy

May I Live with Ease of Heart

and with Balance

You may find a recording of this meditation at www.vimeo.com/greenheartliving

I had the pleasure of attending a retreat at Kripalu led by Sharon Salzberg and Krishna Das, the focus of which was Loving-Kindness. The meditation above is an adaptation of the traditional meditation I learned at the retreat. Sharon Salzberg's book "The Kindness Handbook" provides an in-depth exploration of this meditation and is an uplifting resource for how we approach all relationships in our lives.

"If we truly loved ourselves, we'd never harm another. That is a truly revolutionary, celebratory mode of self-care." - Sharon Salzberg

Green Heart Practice:

Green Heart Pose

A Practice in Gratitude

In our society, we spend a vast majority of our time leaning forward at desks, hovering over a computer, sitting in a car, or riding on trains. All of this leads us to come into a slumped over position, with our shoulders creeping up to our ears. We are embodying our culture's obsession with leaning forward into what's next, rather than experiencing what is.

The Green Heart pose can work miracles to counteract this. Physiologically, this pose does wonders for our bodies, our breath, and our spirits. If you take five minutes a day in this pose, you will feel a difference in your posture and well-being.

If at first this feels wildly uncomfortable, go easy. When I first started my yoga teacher training I had to practice itty bitty backbends. I lay with a little beany baby or tiny pillow under my back. I had so embodied a forward, protective pose, as if it could shield me from the world, that just a small backbend was challenge enough for me.

To come into Green Heart Pose, you are going to lay down on

your back with some supports. You will place supports (a rolled up blanket or pillow) underneath your shoulder blades and under your knees. Adjust your pillows and blankets so that your heart is slightly higher than your head. If it feels too intense on your neck, place a small pillow or blanket underneath the back of your head.

As you hold the pose, release your body into the supports. Take on a balanced breath, letting the breath in and breath out be the same length, and breathe deeply into the ribs.

As you hold this pose, your mind will go all over the place. This is natural. In yoga, we call this the "monkey mind". It likes to jump around and chatter endlessly. Whenever we notice our mind hopping around like a chattering monkey, feel grateful we noticed it and for developing that level of awareness. Feel grateful for the beauty of this moment and come back to your breath.

Tip: Before beginning, pick some soothing music that lasts the length of time you'd like to lay down (5 or 10 minutes). Though you may feel compelled to check your watch, remember there is no need. When the song is over, you know you've completed your time with the pose.

Bonus practice: Whenever you catch your mind wandering, think of one more expression of gratitude. These can be small moments, or big moments. It can be your children, or it can be having found a quarter in the dryer while doing your laundry. This is especially helpful for days when you have a very active, curious mind that is going all over the place.

"If the only prayer you ever say in your life is "thank you", it will be enough." - Meister Eckhart

GREEN HEART PRACTICE:

THE GREEN HEART 7

A PRACTICE IN COMPASSION

These are seven practices that I've found to keep me healthy and feeling good. I am not a nutritionist or a doctor, so please get yourself over to one of those for more specific guidance.

1. Drink warm water with lemon first thing in the morning.

2. Start the day with a few minutes of reflection, meditation and/or writing. Whatever works for you, take at least 3 minutes before looking at your phone or jumping into the day's tasks.

3. Move around each day. Find something you love and do it! Dancing, making love, walking your dog, restorative yoga, power yoga, walking to a friend's house, bicycling. Literally anything. Find a natural movement that makes you smile. Yes, dancing around like a crazy person in your kitchen totally counts.

4. Eat mostly fruits and vegetables. Don't eat things you

can't pronounce, specifically the chemicals and other mumbo-jumbo you'll find in processed and packaged food.

5. Spend time outside in nature every day. If it's truly, desperately miserable out, care for plants inside, look at pictures of trees and wilderness, or listen and deeply enjoy the sound of rain. Our body and souls crave nature.

6. Tune in and drop out. Eliminate or reduce things that stress you out or feel unhealthy for you. (See page 111 for a more detailed version of this practice).

7. Get enough sleep. The amount of sleep needed varies for every person, but most people require 7-8 hours of sleep. Some need less, some need more. Schedule a regular bedtime and wind-down time. After fighting this for 38 years, finally realizing the value of a truly restful night of sleep is a life-altering, beautiful discovery.

Green Heart Practice:
Chakra Reset Meditation
Practice in Abundance

Chakras are energy-centers in our body. Long valued in Eastern medicine, chakras are becoming more and more accepted into Western medicine. Through breath and visualization, this practice will help you find balance in the energy centers in your body. This balance will lead to a healthier, rested body that is more at ease.

Sit comfortably or lay down. Imagine the color red at your tailbone. Call to mind the phrase, "I have". Take 5-10 breaths. Move up to your public bone, imagining the color orange. Think the phrase, "I create". Again, take 5-10 breaths. Move up through the body, taking 5-10 breaths at each chakra.

At your belly button, imagine the color yellow and the phrase "I can." At your heart chakra, imagine the color green and think the phrase, "I love". Light blue graces your throat, with the phrase "I speak". Shift your focus to your third eye, the point between your eyebrows, and imagine it vibrating with the color royal blue and the phrase "I know". Imagine deep violet radiating from your crown chakra, just above the top of your head, and think the phrase "I understand".

Imagine a white light surrounding your body, holding you close. Feel an abundance of this white light swirling around the body, weaving through the cells of the body with each breath. Bring the hands out to the side of the body, opening the palms, ready to receive the healing, balancing power of this energy. You will feel the colors of the chakras expand and lessen, grow and dissipate. Allow the white, shimmering light to bring the chakras to balance. Stay here at least a minute; open to receive. You can access a recording of this practice here: www.vimeo.com/greenheartliving

"Affirmations are our mental vitamins, providing the supplementary positive thoughts we need to balance the barrage of negative events and thoughts we experience daily." - Tia Walker

2 WORK

"Work is love made visible." - Kahlil Gibran, The Prophet

"I always wondered why somebody didn't do something about that. Then I realized I was somebody."- Lily Tomlin

Often in this wild Western world, when we meet people we sum up the whole of our existence by saying what our occupation is. When we are told not to do that, we often resort to saying we're a mother, a daughter, a sister, a brother, a husband, or a wife. Our response shifts to what we are in relationship to others. This is beautiful in that it shows our dedication and the importance we place on our relationships. However, this response is still very distant from who we truly are.

Who are we in the our moments alone? If we sit by ourselves in stillness, who are we? What makes us tick?

When we look at who we are holistically, all our parts, including the things we may judge as dark or light, good or bad, and befriend all of these, we are better able to rock out our life's purpose and to care for our families, our fellow humans, and the earth. The practices learned in the last chapter will prepare you to do this. This chapter focuses on work, including our jobs, and our life's purpose. It includes the work we accomplish in our days that when threaded together create our lives.

I have had at least twenty jobs over the course of my life, but my work goes even beyond those jobs to include volunteer work, service to others and my children, family and animals, and time I have dedicated to art, theater and gardening. This is all work and should be equally valued when considering how we are using our time and energy.

Look back and reflect. How have you spent your days? What have you done?

In my childhood and early adulthood, I was raised in a religion that highly valued a door-to-door ministry. In order for me to be approved of by God, I believed I had to tell others about him. In order for them to be saved from a dismal future, a very scary death, I had to warn them.

This was very real to me as a child. I took my mission seriously. As a result, I spent a great deal of time knocking on doors, having them shut in my face and being yelled at. I spent nights feeling sick to my stomach that I wasn't doing enough. I felt that people would die because I hadn't told them. I thought I would die because I hadn't told enough people.

At 20 years of age, I decided that path was not for me. I still felt compelled to save the world, but shifted my way of doing that to figuring out how to fix it and doing it myself. I felt compelled to take action politically, environmentally, and socially. I felt like I was God's hands on earth and I needed to jump in and solve what was broken. I'd also developed an expectation that people would yell at me, be unhappy to see me, and that most people were not good. I had heard whispers that people in "the world" were out for themselves, devious and would try anything – even being nice – to lure me to their ways.

I spent my early twenties trying to figure out how I could save us from a man-made mass destruction, which seemed imminent. I tried all the things. I worked at a residential program for teenagers, taught art in urban housing projects, bought strangers shoes, and bought my fellow students far too many meals and drinks. I did theater about domestic violence and volunteered at domestic violence shelters. I formed peace groups and marched in rallies in DC, NYC and Hartford. I marched in rallies in support of campaign finance reform, universal health care, and marriage equality. I spent my days and evenings saving the world and my nights drunk. The world was too upsetting, the need too great, my own mind running a million miles an hour, a guilt towering over me. I needed to numb it out.

When I had my kids, I would put them to sleep and drink immediately thereafter. I drank to numb out the overwhelming fear that the world was collapsing and I wasn't doing enough to make it better. Nothing I did seemed enough. Or right. I felt weighed down by guilt, an elusive burden, an unsolvable brokenness.

My children brought a light to my life. It was because of them that I made the choice to see the good in the world and to do what I needed to do to be healthy for them. In honesty, I don't know if I would have made that shift were it not for them. I can imagine my life as a continuously crafted misery; my angst at the world like a fine art peace. Ultimately, it was a choice I made to live life differently. A choice which is available to anyone at any time.

I definitely had some mental and physical health things going on that were contributing towards this plague of overwhelm and despair that have consumed most of my life. Once I started getting enough sleep and making some other physical changes in my life, the elusive, plaguing guilt and despair began to lift. I thought it was very real. I hadn't realized how much caring for my physical body altered my mental state and thoughts. Partnering with a healthcare professional on your self-care can make a world of difference.

There were three things that I needed to change in order to

find joy in my life, while keeping my mission of saving the world.

First, I wasn't loving or caring for myself, so nothing I did would feel right or enough.

Second, I wasn't matching the world's needs with things I actually loved doing, was good at, or was passionate about. I was seeing a need and scrambling around trying to figure out how to solve it, whether I enjoyed solving it or not.

Third, I was pretending I knew the answers and I had it figured out. I was not being vulnerable or open to receive answers. What was a leader after all, but someone who had it all figured out and led others across a finish line to a clear victory? I had imagined the victory as a beautiful, loving world and I would lead the way!

I hadn't realized that the victory was already around me. The victory was the people alongside me I was trying to lead. The beautiful, loving world I thought I was running and leading towards, could only be created by slowing down, looking around, and deeply connecting with those around me in the present moment.

If you are reading this, you are probably driven to make the world a better place. You may have a clear vision of how to do that, or you may not. You may have lost yourself and your joy in life by spending your energies solving the world's problems. You might have thought you had to sacrifice your passions and your love in order to help the world. Or you may have thought that what you really love isn't marketable and can't be what you actually do for a living. You may feel stuck in a job or an occupation that doesn't fulfill your soul, knowing you have a greater gift to share.

If any of these speak to you, you are not alone. Don't give up. I am pleased to tell you that you CAN follow your passion, your purpose, care for your needs and your family, and light up the world in the process. You can do these things by first 1) finding your life's purpose, and 2) resolving to let love be your guide in all of life's choices and actions.

Finding Your Life's Purpose

When discovering our life's purpose or work, also called our dharma, three questions arise: 1) What do we love to do? 2) What are we good at? and 3) What does the world need?

What is critically important is to find an intersection between the three. I really adore watching Murder She Wrote. While I have a deep affection for J. B. Fletcher's adventures in the quaint and beautiful Cabot Cove, Maine, I don't know that the world needs me to view it. Nor would I find it terribly fulfilling as my sole pursuit.

The world needs people to go out in ambulances and patch people up and rescue them. As someone who freezes in the midst of crisis, the world doesn't need me to do that either. So, while the world has a great need for people to save others in emergencies, I am clearly not the best lady for the job.

The beautiful combination of finding things we are good at, enjoy doing, and that the world needs, is our dharma. Now I might be good at something but it makes me sad, or feels tedious. That isn't my dharma. Our dharma lights us up and drives us. The beauty is that when these align, our hearts are full, the world benefits, and we draw the means towards us to continue following our path.

Deepak Chopra speaks exquisitely on the Law of Dharma, sanskrit for "purpose in life", in "The Seven Spiritual Laws of Success":

"The field of pure potentiality is divinity in its essence, and the divine

takes human form to fulfill a purpose. According to this law, you have a unique talent and a unique way of expressing it. There is something that you can do better than anyone else in the whole world - and for every unique talent and unique expression of that talent, there are also unique needs. When these needs are matched with the creative expression of your talent, that is the spark that creates affluence. Expressing your talents to fulfill needs creates unlimited wealth and abundance."

By using your talents and your gifts to fulfill a need in the world, you will light up your own life and heal the world in the process.

Choose From Love

The second key to greening our work is learning to let love be our guiding principle in all our choices. I had a rough lesson when I realized that often in the working world, I was not choosing from love. I was always the one to jump in and offer to take something on. It didn't matter if I didn't have time, didn't know how to do it, or felt overwhelmed by the prospect. If it needed doing, I was your Gal Friday.

For years, I was in a repetitive pattern of being overwhelmed. I would take on too much, go into a bit of chaos, try to pretend I wasn't, eventually the chaos would win, I would let people down, I would let myself down, I would beat myself up, collapse, give up… and then slowly pick up the pieces again as if nothing had happened.

This felt like an inevitable part of my personality. It was a disappointing flaw in my character that I wore like a badge of honor. *'I am the person that will take on too much! I will get things done. If you want the rockstar, you also have to deal with the crushing collapse that comes with it.'*

It wasn't until my 38th year on this planet, after six months of Life Coach and Leadership Training under my belt, that I learned a life-altering thing about myself. I realized this pattern wasn't inevitable. And that it was a choice. This was not a character flaw. It was a choice I made over and over. And I could choose something wildly different.

This pattern had caused me and those around me plenty of minor, annoying consequences (i.e. being late to everything all the time and often having multiple things scheduled for the same time.) It has caused me to suffer panic attacks and stress-related physical ailments. Worse, it has also caused life threatening consequences, including a car accident, the loss of a job, and what I will gently call a nervous breakdown.

Realizing this was not who I was… that I had a choice …. that I could stop anywhere in this pattern and make a different choice …. was life changing.

But how could I change it? How could I stop myself from taking on too much?

First, I had to learn why I was taking everything on. I realized I was very attached to this idea of being a bit of a Wonder Woman. Oh, this needs doing? I'll save you! (I don't know how to use this software but I'll figure it out! I've never written a state grant but I'll learn on the job and start with one that has million-dollar consequences and involves 12 agencies!)

Yes, part of this was in service of the greater good, as I was working for nonprofits with important missions. But I had to admit, a part of me was being a little showy-offy. (Oh, I can learn it… look how much I can DO!)

Who wants that attitude? Who wants to be around someone who feels the need to prove they can one-up everyone?

That is definitely not acting out of love, in multiple ways. 1) The motivation is a little snarky and show-offy, even if it's for a good purpose. 2) By taking on things that were way above my capability, available time, knowledge, or current skill-set I was putting other things at risk. By not being honest about my ability to manage something, I ended up causing others suffering when there were breakdowns and I couldn't deliver. 3) My well-being, my family, and my sleep all suffered, which was not showing love for myself.

It is true that I've learned lots of new things by having this attitude. I've learned so much by just diving in and believing I could do things. There is a value in that, both for myself and for my employers, and the communities I've served. However, to the extent that this has contributed to my getting overwhelmed and sinking into an unhealthy cycle, this is asking for burnout. Burnout helps no one. If you keep taking on too much and stress is ever present, you feel anxious over work or feel like you are in a rat race, take on the following practices to help shift out of the cycle.

GREEN HEART PRACTICE:

CHOOSE LOVE

A PRACTICE IN COMPASSION

This practice is simply to ask this question "Am I choosing love?" whenever we are presented with a choice.

Find the spaces and times in your life when you often take on "one more thing". Is it through phone conversations, on Facebook, at staff meetings, or in your kitchen? Wherever you make that decision, write down or post, "Am I choosing from love?" Allow yourself space to consider it before taking something on.

If someone asks you a question, pause. Give yourself permission to take some time to decide. This may look like saying, "I'm not sure that I can commit to that right now. I have something to check up on. I will let you know by the end of today."

There is no need to give an excuse or a reason not to do something. Respond flatly. "I won't be doing that today, but thank you for including me." No reason is needed.

If this is hard for you, choose to do this as an example for others of how to be in the world. Your firm commitment to choose love for others as well as yourself sets a beautiful example. You can lead the way with each interaction and decision in which you choose LOVE.

"I believe that every single event in life is an opportunity to choose love over fear." - Oprah Winfrey

GREEN HEART PRACTICE:

DAILY GREENS

A PRACTICE IN GRATITUDE

Daily Greens is a four-part free-writing exercise that can take 5-20 minutes. It is incredibly helpful to do at the beginning of the day to get the day off to a fresh and clear start.

Take out a clean sheet of paper and complete written responses to each of these prompts:

- **Free Write -** Write down anything that is worrying you, stressing you out, or feels like a burden. Take as long as you need to write it out. Once you are done, ask yourself, is there anything else? Keep writing until you get it all out.

- **Greening -** In what ways are you growing? Where are you seeing abundance in your life? This can be in any area, including family, relationships, work, or money. Even if an area is not perfect, write about anything that is going right, anything that you have learned from and grown from, anything that feels like a shift towards your most authentic, highest self.

- **Practice** - Write about anything that you want to set as a practice for the day. Rather than something to check off, one and done, this is something to keep exploring. It can often be helpful to phrase it as a question. For instance, "Am I choosing from Love?" "Does this align with my mission/life purpose?" "Do I need to be the one to do this?" are all questions that can serve in preventing overwhelm and burnout and help you keep priorities in focus and your heart and body healthy.

- **Intention** - This can be a mantra, a word, a phrase or an image. Something which will call you back to yourself. Mine is often simply LOVE, which is my life's purpose. Think of it as a seed that you would want to plant in your heart and being for the day. Choose something that helps you feel lighter and more hopeful.

"When you are grateful, fear disappears and abundance appears."
- Anthony Robbins

3 HOME

"The ache for home lives in all of us. The safe place we can go as we are and not be questioned." - Maya Angelou

"Where we love is home, home that our feet may leave, but not our hearts." - Oliver Wendell Holmes Sr.

Home can be a space in your heart as well as a tangible place. It can mean where we rest our head at night and also the places we spend most of our day, our workplace/office, our car, the train, the places we walk, play, and eat. Everywhere we spend our days, and everything that supports our life is our home. Reach out beyond the offices, the houses, the school, and extend our sense of home to the farms that feed us, the rivers and watersheds that water those crops, the forests that breathe oxygen into the air that reach our lungs. What if we began thinking of it all as our home? What if we approached our surroundings and felt deep love for all of it?

We will begin our exploration of home by looking at our physical home where we rest our heads and extend our focus to include all the aspects of home in our life.

Where We Rest Our Head

A scary thing happened after I got separated from my children's father and was living on my own. The kids were with their dad 3 days a week, so there were 3 days where I was in the house by myself. Suddenly, there was no one I could blame for the house being a wreck, for the garage door not working, for the lawn not being mowed, for the piles of paper, and laundry. It was literally all on me. This was extremely disheartening. A

70-year old house with two acres of land was (and is) a lot to keep on my shoulders.

I learned quickly that I needed support, but it took me a long time to learn how to ask for it.

On Clearing Out the Garage and My Soul

For over a year I couldn't pull a car into my garage. It was filled with furniture that was destroyed by a cat, junk that had been left by the previous owner, and many broken things. Lack of time and money were the excuse, as well as not wanting to ask for help. It caused me great anxiety, shame and overwhelm.

For the benefit of the reader, I will now share several lessons I learned here: 1) Require that previous owners remove all their belongings and debris before moving out. Once you move in, there's a definite possibility it won't budge for a decade. 2) Don't buy the thing. Just don't. My overflowing garage included more things than I care to mention that I used once and then broke. These were a waste of money, space, and energy. 3) When people leave things at your house, contact them and have an expectation that they pick it up by a certain date or it will mysteriously disappear. To be fully transparent, this is a "do as I say and not as I do" peice of advice. 4) Don't ever take in a fourth cat. When you feel tempted, imagine cleaning cat urine off a piano and a garage filled with reeking couches.

Once the garage got to the can't-pull-a-car-in-therefore -rendering-the-garage-without-purpose-level, I developed a beautiful plan to organize friends and family to help me clear it out, borrow my dad's van, and bring it to the dump.

This seemed like a perfectly achievable plan, but for some reason it just didn't happen. For whatever reason this brilliant plan remained in my head. I came up with excuses. I was always busy. I didn't want to ask for help. It seemed overwhelming. I stalled and stalled.

Fortunately, I had two assets that could slay all of those excuses: a very strong boyfriend and a debit card.

One day I said ENOUGH. I ordered a dumpster and in a week, Michael and I worked together to fill that baby up.

I had expected a blessed wave of relief to wash over me. A chorus of HALLELUJAH expounding from the heavens. Freedom from the mess! A giant hug from the universe, my guardian angel to come on in and say, "You did it! Good job."

At the very least, a smile on my face and a lightness. A relief.

Instead, when the garage was emptied, and the dumpster was pretty much overflowing, I lay down on the couch and cried for 2 hours straight.

What was THAT about?

So much.

After I let go of beating myself up for feeling bad over a good thing, I began sorting out what seemed like a bizarre reaction.

Turns out, I felt a lot of anger and disappointment in myself that I had let it get like that in the first place. And that I had carried this worry, this burden around with me like an anchor. For a whole year.

And in the end it had taken 2 people, a couple day's worth of my paycheck and a few days of lifting and moving gross things. And it was DONE.

When I compared the energy I had expended towards this in anticipation, blame, and planning, with the energy it took to actually do something about it, the vast difference knocked me out and rendered me weeping on the couch. As if, perhaps, to make up for some of the difference.

What are you carrying around? What is an anchor that you are dragging around? What is holding you back? These anchors can show up anywhere in our lives, but are often most present and weighty at home.

There can be benefit in investigating the why. How is having that burden serving you? Why aren't you choosing to be done with it? Has it benefited you in some way? Has it served as an excuse, a reminder, a tale of woe, an object for complaint? Figuring this out could teach you a lot about yourself. If it shows up in one place in your life, chances are it will keep showing up until you notice it and deal with it.

Of equal value to investigating the meaning, is to just take care of it. If something is bothering you and feels like a burden, you have a decision. You can 1) take action to do something about it, 2) decide to keep carrying it around without complaint, or 3) decide to keep carrying it around with complaint. Know in your heart that whatever is happening is a decision you are choosing. It's not something that's happened to you. You are deciding it.

I could very well have blamed my garage on many other people, but at the end it was on me. For a while, the value of keeping the anchor around my neck with complaint, seemed ok. Once the value of using the garage as a complaint against all fourth cats and all the other people I had expected to help me empty it but didn't, my complaints seemed empty. I couldn't find the value in keeping the anchor without the complaint. I decided to finally take action.

It may feel icky to realize that we are holding on to things to use them as complaints or excuses, rallying against wrongs and injustices, pointing to lessons learned or false reasons for why we can't do other things. Trust that if you've stepped into a place that feels icky, there could also be a beautiful opportunity for change and growth.

Consider that when we are presented with a problem, our mind will generally follow one of four directions: 1) Blame, 2) Creating a magical solution, 3) Shutting down, or 4) Taking ownership.

In blaming, we feel frustration around someone else that we think should have done the thing that isn't done. We can also blame ourselves and spend time feeling awful about how something isn't done and just stay in that space. I spent a lot of time with my garage in "blame", both blaming others and myself.

In creating a magical solution, we develop an inviting fantasy of some savior that's going to swoop in and fix the problem. One of my magical solutions was that people would come help me clear out my garage. The day was unspecified and the request went unasked, so it remained in fantasy-land.

In shutting down, we may feel overwhelmed and give up on the task, ignore it, and often numb out in some way to pretend the problem isn't there. In the case of my garage, I spent plenty of time (a year) ignoring the problem and thinking my television, my work, or literally *anything else*, was way more important.

In taking ownership, we develop a plan to fix the problem. and follow through. This might take the form of deciding to fix it ourselves or call in reinforcements to help. Both are taking ownership. Taking ownership doesn't mean doing everything yourself. It means deciding that you will take action to fix the problem. Taking action might include communicating to your partner or roommate that you have been expecting them to do the dishes, but you hadn't ever let them in on the expectation. It could mean sitting down with them and talking about what things need to be done in the house and to work together to make a plan to make that happen. This might also include calling in other people to help if it is something neither of you can manage. In the case of my garage, taking action included researching dumpster companies, asking for someone to help, deciding on a timeframe that would work for both of us, calling and reserving the dumpster, creating time the week it was here to clear out the garage, and taking the final step of throwing everything into it.

It can be challenging to realize we are blaming, creating magical solutions, or shutting down in the moment. All of these things feel very real. 'The dishes AREN'T done and it is HER FAULT!' feels very real at the time. Imagining getting a roommate who is very enthusiastic about doing the dishes is a deeply engaging fantasy. Facebook becomes incredibly fascinating when compared to the pile of dishes in the sink.

These all feel very real and are incredibly captivating in the moment. It can take a lot of practice to realize what they are. These are letting the world happen TO us, rather than happen BY us. It can take practice to realize that we can take ownership of our lives and to develop the commitment and ability to take action around every aspect of our life. The Green Heart Practices that follow are an excellent place to start.

Green Heart Practice:

Taking Ownership

Practice in Compassion

For a week, notice how you are reacting to things that need doing at home. Examples include: dirty windows that need cleaning, dishes piling in the sink, or grass growing higher in the yard.

What thoughts come into mind?

Our mind will generally follow one of four directions: 1) Blame, 2) Creating a magical solution, 3) Shutting down, or 4) Taking ownership.

To start this practice, begin noticing how you are reacting. Are you reacting with Blame, Looking for a Magical Solution, Shutting Down or Taking Ownership? Begin practicing choosing where you are coming from.

I have yet to meet the person who is ready to take ownership of everything 100% of the time. It is perfectly acceptable to let yourself fantasize for a few minutes about the perfect partner who loves to do the laundry. It is equally perfect to put off the raking and let yourself shut down and watch a TV show for an hour. Notice, however, how much time you are spending in each of these. Recognize each of these as a choice. Decide where you want to choose from.

"Love doesn't just sit there, like a stone. It has to be made, like bread; remade all the time, like new." - Ursula K. Le Guin

Green Heart Practice:

Fait Accomplit!

Practice in Gratitude

At the beginning of the week, make a list of all the things that need to be done in the home. Only write down things that you are having trouble doing and that feel BIG. For instance, if I had 2 loads of laundry to do that I knew I'd get to in the next couple of days, I wouldn't write it down. However, if I have 7 loads of laundry in the basement and the thought of it made me want to curl up and hide like a pair of warn-in socks, I'd write it on the list. (Of note: This is not an opportunity to beat yourself up! The list might feel overwhelming but trust the process.)

Make two lists: Fait Accomplit! and Complete. As a practice, take on moving one thing in your Fait Accomplit! list over to Complete each day. Make it a priority to do that first.

At the beginning of the day, choose ONE thing from your Fait Accomplit! list that you are going to take action on today. Fait Accomplit means "as good as done". See yourself taking the steps to get that completed. What will it take? If you don't know exactly, see yourself asking someone else for help and them helping you. Imagine it being complete. This thing is as good as done. You can trust that it will happen. At the end of each day, look at your list. Did you accomplish your target today? Write either "in progress" or "complete" next to the item. If you didn't accomplish it, don't give up. You will get it done. Remember, it's as good as done, just needing a few actions on your part to bring it to fruition. No stress, no overwhelm, just resolve, and placing one foot in front of the other will get you there.

At the end of the week, look at your list and feel the lightness around moving things forward. Allow a feeling of gratitude towards yourself for making the commitment to making that happen.

If there were things you didn't get done, again, do not beat yourself up. Feel grateful for the opportunity to carry it forward. At the end of the month take a look. If things are progressively being moved forward instead of being accomplished, (painting the bathroom ceiling, fixing the door, a leaky sink), this is telling you to call in reinforcements.

Ask yourself what is stopping you from asking for help? (Money, time, etc....) Get curious about that. Ask what it could mean to just do the thing. What lightness would that create in your life? Ask for help. If money is an obstacle - ask friends for help or become determined to create additional income to cover the cost. Or you might have something you can barter. Often friends and family want to help, but don't know what to do. Consider what it would mean for you to have this done and resolve to find a way.

This list can be used for all of our environments, not just our home. We can put it to use in our work, our businesses, our wellness goals and our relationships. We can waste a lot of energy on feelings of uncertainty, confusion and overwhelm. This practice can add a lightness to our life and speed up the process that things get done.

"I am thankful for a lawn that needs mowing, windows that need cleaning and gutters that need fixing because it means I have a home."

- Nancie J. Carmody

GREEN HEART PRACTICE:

GREEN YOUR HOME

PRACTICE OF COMPASSION

These 7 practices create a greener, healthier home.

1) **Love Up Your Home -** Instead of looking as it as a chore, approach cleaning, repairs, and maintenance of your home as an expression of LOVE for it.

2) **All Hands on Deck -** Everyone who lives in the home does their part to take care of it. Even young children can help.

3) **Plant a Garden -** In the words of Mahatma Gandhi, "To forget how to dig the earth and to tend the soil is to forget ourselves." Few things are as healing as planting seeds and watching them grow.

4) **Make Your Own Cleaners -** Cheaper, better for the earth, and makes cleaning slightly more interesting.

5) **Art and Music -** Every home is better with art and music, your own and that created by others.

6) **Eat Local Food -** Support local farms and grow your own.

7) **Reduce, Reuse, Recycle** - Less stuff is good for the earth and everyone's sanity.

Green Heart Practice:
The Elephant in the Room
Practice of Gratitude

Do you have a special image or symbol that calls you back to yourself? For me it's elephants. I have been fond of elephants my whole life. I have a beautiful memory of visiting Lucy the Elephant in Margate and a special fondness for Babar. (So much so that my daughter's middle name is Celeste, in part after Queen Celeste, the elephant queen). When I began studying yoga, I was beyond thrilled to learn of Ganesha, an elephant-headed deity, the remover of obstacles, a symbol of power and change. Images of elephants always call me back to myself. They help me remember that even when things seem impossible for me, there's a force greater than myself that can help clear it out. When I was going through separation and divorce, the images of elephants were deeply calming to me. I felt the world on my shoulders and seeing the image of an elephant would remind me I had help to carry that weight. Elephants reminded me that even though I felt tiny and puny compared to my challenges, no obstacle was too large.

What is your elephant? What is something you need to be

reminded, that lifts the weight of the world off your shoulders? Find an image that can provide this for you. I love the power of animals, but it could be something else for you, a word, a photograph of a very special place where you felt perfectly serene. Place these images where you spend a lot of time - your many homes - your house, your work, your car. This will help you remember you are not alone, that even if we can't figure things out on our own, that doesn't mean they are insurmountable.

"Be easy. Take your time. You are coming home. To yourself."
- Nayyirah Waheed

GREEN HEART PRACTICE:

COMING HOME

A PRACTICE IN GRATITUDE

Come into child's pose. Kneel on a yoga mat, or a bed, put a blanket on top of our heels and sit on it. Your forehead can rest on a bolster or pile of pillows. Hold for 3-5 minutes, turn your head to the other side halfway through. To find a demonstration of this pose and meditation, go to vimeo.com/greenheartliving

Allow the breath to become a balanced breath, with the breath in and the breath in being the same length. Breath in and out through your nose.

Add the mantra "I Am". On the breath in, think "I" and on the breath out, think "Am". Notice what comes up when you first introduce the thought I Am. Notice without judgement. I am…. safe, home, enough, perfect, LOVE. Ground your awareness with safe, positive assurances.

Of note, after thinking the thought "I am", many people will automatically go into a barrage of awful things they are. (Ex: I am a mess, I am sad, I am a disappointment, I am a failure.) For years, this was what played in my head. This practice, in addition to calming us and bringing us home, can do wonders to reprogram the mind, to replace the negative playback with peace and contentment. If negative thoughts creep in, come back to the mantra and replace the negative thoughts with affirmations, such as "I am enough", "I am love", or "I am courageous".

You can also use the Sankrit phrase "So Hum", which means "I am" and mirrors the sound of our breath, our life force.

"To meditate means to go home to yourself. Then you know how to take care of the things that are happening inside you, and you know how to take care of the things that happen around you." - Thich Nhat Hanh

4 Love

"Something amazing happens when we surrender and just love. We melt into another world, a realm of power already within us. The world changes when we change. The world loves us when we choose to love the world."
- Marianne Williamson

"Being deeply loved by someone gives you strength, while loving someone deeply gives you courage." - Lao Tzu

Love is most commonly thought of as an emotion or a feeling. Love is something that happens to us or sweeps us away; something we get caught up in. Love also takes action and can be a choice. Love can be a way to view the world and a way to navigate our choices.

Answering Love's Call

In Kahlil Gibran's "The Prophet", a crowd asks the prophet Almitra to speak to them of love. His response:

"When love beckons to you follow him, Though his ways are hard and steep...And when he speaks to you believe in him, Though his voice may shatter your dreams as the north wind lays waste the garden."

There is no promise that love is easy or will go as you have envisioned it, but it is most important that we answer its call. It is important to step into love and let it guide us and shape us, despite our fears.

The prophet Almitra further explained to the crowd:

"If in your fear you would seek only love's peace and love's pleasure, Then it is better for you that you...pass out of love's threshing floor, Into the seasonless world where you shall laugh, but not all of your laughter, and

weep, but not all of your tears."

Many people live a life protecting themselves from harm. They shut off their feelings of love out of a fear of losing it. They limit their experience of love in all its joy and beauty, too afraid of being vulnerable. They build armor around themselves in an attempt to keep their hearts from being broken. They end up breaking their hearts with their own armor. The fortresses they've built around themselves to protect themselves from embarrassment or pain, can end up crushing their own inner light, and full expression of life. Acting from love is a frightening choice and is not for the faint of heart, but acting consistently from love brings a life of beauty, grace, spirit, and possibility.

Love > Fear

Fear is a warden and the majority of humans are its prisoner, regardless of recognition of this or not. Allowing love to be your guiding principle in life is the key to possibility, connection and relief. It is the key to clearing out feelings of overwhelm and fear.

John Lennon beautifully described the power of fear and love to shape our world in this way:

"There are two basic motivating forces: fear and love. When we are afraid, we pull back from life. When we are in love, we open to all that life has to offer with passion, excitement, and acceptance. We need to learn to love ourselves first, in all our glory and our imperfections. If we cannot love ourselves, we cannot fully open to our ability to love others or our potential to create. Evolution and all hopes for a better world rest in the fearlessness and open-hearted vision of people who embrace life."

By choosing to be motivated by love rather than fear, we are creating a better world for us all. If we have spent a lifetime being motivated by fear, it can take some time to shift to being primarily motivated by love. Treat yourself gently as you practice choosing from love more and more. Over time being motivated by love will come more naturally and it will begin to feel odd to choose from any other place.

When I am scared to talk to someone, fear can easily shut me down. When I intentionally choose to let love take leadership and guide the interaction, my fear can be overcome. Love can remove my fear of saying the wrong thing, worrying over whether or not someone will like me, or all the bad things that could happen if I let my guard down. When I remember that all that matters in any interaction with another human is connection and relationship, fear is cast outside.

When I catch myself being nervous to talk with someone and I choose to shift into thinking about it from a perspective of love, my entire approach and feelings change. I'm no longer controlled by fear or anxiety. Fear and anxiety might still be present, but it's no longer as important. It doesn't rule the day. Being led by love allows a relief from attachment to results, whether or not the other person will like me, or how things should "go". When I let love guide the interaction and step out of my own way, not only does a huge burden lift from off my shoulders, but everything always seems to go much better.

Leading With Love

Letting love guide our interactions and choices brings tremendous clarity to life and helps us where we might get in our own way. Understanding the different forms love can take helps us to use love in every interaction.

C.S. Lewis's "The Four Loves" explores the nature of love as defined by the Greeks. Lewis elaborates on four categories of love: Storge, Philia, Eros and Agape. Storge is familial love and is based on natural affection, such as that a mother would have for a child. Philia is friendship and includes relationships based around a common goal or a shared enthusiasm. Eros is sexual and passionate, most closely related to romantic love. Agape is universal or spiritual love. It is the most unselfish of the loves and has also been defined as "charity".

Agape includes acting from love without expecting anything in return. It includes demonstrating kindness and showing acts of service to people that might be considered unlovable, ugly or undeserving. It includes the love of strangers, nature and the divine. Even on days when we don't feel terribly loving, we can still allow love to be a choice we can make. We can choose to lead with acts of service, compassion, and kindness, rooted in Agape, universal love.

Love, in all its forms, is the root of life, and the reason for it. It is how all things have come to be and exist. To turn our back on love is to turn our back on ourselves.

Green Heart Practice:
A Week of Worldview
Practice in Compassion

This practice is a week-long practice, with an opportunity to try on a new practice of worldview each day. Apply it to all interactions with people: with your children, your parents, your boss, your colleagues, your coworkers, your staff, your friends, strangers, people at the grocery store, etc... Incorporate the value of "sakshin" or witnessing. See if you can jump out of each interaction enough to view it outside yourself, and observe the interaction at a bit of a distance.

Day 1 Listening: While talking to someone else, notice how often you are preparing your next response. As my Aunt Ginny once exclaimed at dinner, "We all think we are talking to each other, but we're really just talking to ourselves."

Day 2 Right/Wrong: How often are you judging and making things right or wrong? How often do you see others making yours or other's actions right or wrong? "They shouldn't have done that.... You should have...."

Day 3 Complaints: How often are you relating to people

through having complaints, hearing complaints, agreeing with complaints, or one-upping their complaints.

Day 4 Ignoring/Avoiding: How often are you avoiding/diving out of conversations that will feel uncomfortable? Do you catch yourself putting on blinders to block out things you don't want to see?

Day 5 Plenty or Not Enough: How often do you or other people say there is "not enough" of something? Where does that show up and what is your reaction? Are there instances where there is plenty or an abundance? Where does that show up and what is your reaction?

Day 6 Control: How often do you make decisions based on your wish to control? (Control can be in any area... controlling people, time, circumstances, etc...) How often do you witness others making decisions that appear to be based on control?

Day 7: Consider that rather than all of the above being Truth, that they may be a framework, a mindset, a lens at which to view the world. Take a moment to reflect about how any of these frameworks or lenses might be limiting? If you could shift your view, even temporarily, what would that make possible?

This might cause some explosions in your mind... *Well he SHOULDN'T have done that!!!! And there ISN'T enough time!!!! ....* Play with the idea of what could be possible in your life by trying on a different viewpoint.

If any of these areas seem to open up a different possibility try on that practice for a day or even a week. Explore how that feels. It might feel wildly uncomfortable at first - you've probably spent a whole lifetime building a worldview - it may take some time to shift it. Another note, it can be very difficult to see our own worldview without assistance - and much easier to see it in others. You could go through this entire worldview practice first viewing it in others - and then over time seeing if you can find it in yourself. If you still have difficulty, ask people around you to help or work with a coach or mentor to see where there might be more possibility in your life that you're not yet able to see.

"Unfortunately in this world of ours, each person views things through a certain medium, which prevents his seeing them in the same light as others."
- Alexandre Dumas, The Count of Monte Cristo

Green Heart Practice:
Love > Fear Meditation
A Practice in Compassion

The next time you feel anxious or fearful of talking with someone take a moment to pause and shift. Get curious about the feeling of fear. What exactly are you afraid of? Where does the feeling of fear reside in your body? Do you feel it in certain places more than others? Take a moment to reflect on these and write them down.

Begin to breath in through your nose to a count of 4 and breath out through your mouth to a count of 6. Let the breath out carry with it anything that is causing you fear or anxiety. On the breath in, breathe in love. Imagine you can breathe love into all the cells of your body. Each breath out is making more space in the body for love. Continue this practice for 3-7 minutes.

You can find a recording of this meditation here: vimeo.com/greenheartliving

"Perfect love throws fear outside." - 1 John 4:18

GREEN HEART PRACTICE:

GRATITUDE JOURNAL

PRACTICE IN GRATITUDE

At the end of each day, write three things down that you are grateful for. These can be very small and simple (a kind word that someone said to you that day or a flower you noticed in your yard) or very large (a child being born or you starting a new business). This is an easy action that will begin to shift your perspective from what is "wrong" in the world, to what is going "right". Keeping it in a journal can create a place you can turn to when life feels down and off. You can read a few pages of your Gratitude Journal to remind you of all you can be thankful for.

"The miracle of gratitude is that it shifts your perception to such an extent that it changes the world you see." - Dr. Robert Holden

GREEN HEART PRACTICE:

KARUNA HUM MEDITATION

PRACTICE IN COMPASSION

In this meditation we will use the mantra "Karuna Hum" to focus our attention and awareness. Karuna means "compassion" and Hum means "I am". By repeating this phrase silently in our mind during meditation, we develop a compassion for all living beings, allowing us to view them as an extension of ourselves.

Sit comfortably and breathe deeply. Repeat the phrase "Karuna Hum" a few times aloud and then allow it to go internal, repeating the phrase silently in your mind. Your mind will wander. Know that this is very natural. When you catch your mind wandering, that is the magical moment you have to draw your awareness back to the mantra. Begin with a practice of 5 minutes and gradually increase to 11 or 20 minutes.

5 Money

"Money is neither my god nor my devil. It is a form of energy that tends to make us more of who we already are, whether it's greedy or loving."
- Dan Millman

"A generous heart filled with gratitude is a magnet for abundance."
- Debasish Meidha

Through my work at the United Way, I have trained and mentored volunteer financial coaches and met with many people who are participants in the financial coaching program. Participants join in an effort to make their families more financially stable, to learn to balance a budget, increase their income, decrease their debts and improve their credit. The financial coaches volunteer their time to give back to their community, one household at a time.

People have different emotional baggage and views around money. The curious thing is that most people think their way is the only way! It is very hard to see your own belief system around money without guidance. There are as many belief systems around money as there are people on the planet.

The belief systems we hold around money are instilled in us from our parents and through our own personal experience. Financial belief systems can be completely at odds with current financial situations. Someone who is wealthy that is terrified of losing their wealth will make decisions around money from a competitive, scarcity mindset, despite having more than enough to meet their needs. Someone who is poor as dirt may give someone the shirt off their back or spend their last dime on someone else, trusting that another shirt or dime is just around the corner.

Judgements abound when it comes to finances. Some people would view spending money on others over themselves as immoral, short-sighted or idiotic. Other people will view people who spend money on themselves instead of others as immoral, short-sighted or idiotic. It is astounding to see the differences from the outside. It is very hard to see our own stories for what they are - historical fiction. Our financial stories may be based on our past or that of our parents or their parents, but the stories are fictions all the same.

We have a relationship with money just like we have a relationship with all other things. Consider the idea that we can choose what type of relationship we have with money and empower that choice. The stories and judgements we have today around money don't need to control the rest of our lives and that of our families.

Stephen Covey, author of "The 7 Habits of Highly Effective People", shares his mindset this way, "I have an abundance mentality: When people are genuinely happy at the successes of others, the pie gets larger." My slice of pie doesn't need to take away from yours. My success doesn't need to take away from yours. With an abundance mindset, there is more than enough to go around. We can work together to make the pie larger for all.

We get to decide whether we want to have a scarcity framework around money, an abundant mindset, or something else entirely.

Coming from an abundant mindset doesn't mean spending money you don't have. Using credit cards when you are not anticipating a way to pay them off is not abundant thinking. In looking at our relationship with money, relying on credit and maxing out credit cards is using money in an abusive way.

There is no benefit in beating yourself up over past choices. If you are currently looking at a mountain of credit card debt or a dismally low credit score, know that you are not alone and that abundance and financial prosperity are still within your reach. As in all areas of our lives, we have to face the consequences of our actions but we get to choose how to do things differently going forward.

My guiding principle to working with money is to have 1) Magic and 2) a Plan. The trouble was, for years and years, I could never do both at the same time. I was either led by the belief that everything would work out by the magic of divine intervention or relying entirely on my own plans. I was either chanting mantras for abundance, praying, and trusting the universe OR carrying the world on my shoulders, planning budgets until after midnight, and waking up in the middle of the night feeling sick over my credit card debt or unpaid bills. I could not find a happy medium.

To be truly financially prosperous, which to me means to have money work in service of your life purpose, you need both Magic and a Plan. The Plan includes: developing a budget, looking for gaps between income and expenses, generating goals for income and expenses, and creating a structure to meet those goals. The Magic includes: believing in your goal, even when you don't exactly know HOW it will work out. It includes allowing the universe to support you in ways that you hadn't envisioned or planned. It means keeping your eyes open and being ready to say "yes, and!" when the universe shows up with a new opportunity we hadn't envisioned. The practices on the following pages provide a means to discover for yourself how to create and implement your own Magic and Plans in regards to money, financial prosperity, and abundance.

GREEN HEART PRACTICE:

BUDGETS (SURVIVALIST, SUSTAINABLE, VISION)

A PRACTICE IN ABUNDANCE

Create three budgets: Survivalist, Sustainable, and Vision.

The Survivalist Budget is what you need to meet your basic needs, including paying off debt and periodic expenses (insurance or property taxes should be divided and spread across months equally). That is what you need to meet your household's basic needs. Where there is a gap between your income and expenses, focus on closing the gap. Where can you decrease or combine expenses? Where can you increase income?

The Sustainable Budget includes saving monthly for when unexpected expenses come up (car or house repair, medical expenses, etc...) Building an emergency savings account is a critical piece of developing a financially stable future. Emergency and unexpected expenses are inevitable and a part of life. They will not be avoided. Having savings available to respond to these inevitabilities will keep them from knocking you too far back. "Pay yourself first" by setting aside a designated amount for savings first, perhaps having it be automatically deposited into a separate savings account.

The Vision Budget is WAY more fun than the others. This includes what income and expenses you will have living the life you really want to be living. This gets the wheels turning for how much you need to draw in to get to where you want to get to.

"The key to abundance is meeting limited circumstances with unlimited thoughts." - Marianne Williamson

Green Heart Practice:

Money Stories

A Practice in Abundance

What is our "story" with money? Does that "story" serve you? How do things usually go? Do you know that others have different stories? That your way isn't the only way. Money holds energy and meaning for many people. It means different things and is used in different ways.

Consider that your story around money is just that, a story. Many of us carry forward a story we were taught or, sometimes, act on the exact opposite of the story we were taught.

You have a choice what your relationship will be with money, regardless of what your story and your relationship has been in the past. You can decide to start this new relationship today.

What relationship do you want to have with money? Here is the relationship that I am choosing now:

Money and I take care of each other. Together we make the world a more beautiful, loving, healthy place. We are always there for each other. We help each other grow.

What would you like your relationship with money to be? Write it out and place it somewhere prominent in your life as a reminder. Some days I realize I've fallen back into my old relationship with money, which felt like playing Tetris, scrambling, and never having enough. Whenever I notice that's happening, I remember that I get to start again. I get to shift into my new money relationship. I get to choose again. And so do you.

"A rich man is nothing but a poor man with money." - W. C. Fields

GREEN HEART PRACTICE:

ABUNDANCE JOURNAL

A PRACTICE IN ABUNDANCE

Each day write down areas where abundance is appearing in your life. Examples include money, food, clothes, gifts, kindnesses, people. This a way of encouraging abundant thought, focusing on the positive, and trusting there is more than enough to go around. It provides fuel to keep going during tough times.

Everything we need to learn we can learn from the earth. Nature is abundant, with countless seeds to every seed that germinates. There is more than enough food for all humans and animals on earth. There is more than enough land for all the humans and animals to live simply in peace. What is limiting? Humans. Humans have chosen to use money as a form of exchange and let that dictate control and the way we exchange energy. Humans control who gets food and who doesn't. Who has a home and who doesn't. Who has land and who doesn't. Humans are controlling and often focus on lack and shortage. What if we shifted our way of being to align more with the abundance of nature?

What if instead of seeing lack and limited resources, we approached the world with the knowledge that there's plenty to go around? What if we saw each venture as a potential partnership, rather than as a potential battle.

Writing daily about where abundance shows up in your life will help cultivate a shift from a mindset of lack and scarcity, to a mindset of abundance.

"Not what we have but what we enjoy constitutes our abundance."

- Epicurus

GREEN HEART PRACTICE:

AHRA KAHRAH MEDITATION

A PRACTICE IN ABUNDANCE

Ahra Kahra is sanskrit for "I Invoke the Creativity of the Universe in My Life". Using this mantra during our meditation practice allows us to welcome the abundant creativity of the universe to partner with us in our life. Set aside 7 minutes each morning for a week and use this mantra as your focal point. Set the intention for the rest of the day to stay alert to what opportunities and abundance shows up in your life. Often opportunities are right in front of us, but we turn a blind eye because they are not what we expected. Notice what shows up and see how you can partner with it.

I was introduced to the "Ahra Kahra" meditation during one of the Chopra Center's 21-day Meditation Experiences. These are free 21-day meditations that are made available periodically online. They are an excellent way to begin or kickstart a meditation practice. You can learn more here: www.chopracentermeditation.com

6 TIME

"Time is a created thing. To say 'I don't have time,' is like saying, 'I don't want to'. - Lao Tzu

"Learn to enjoy every minute of your life. Be happy now. Don't wait for something outside of yourself to make you happy in the future. Think how really precious is the time you have to spend, whether it's at work or with your family. Every minute should be enjoyed and savored."
- Earl Nightingale

Oh, sweet, elusive time. Even though we all have the same minutes in a day and hours in a year, time seems to drag out or speed up entirely based on what we are doing. Time flies when we are having fun and drags when we are bored. When we have a looming deadline, time can seem like a cruel task master, speeding up and freaking us out. If we are waiting for a pot to boil so we can throw our spaghetti noodles in it or are waiting in line, a much shorter amount of time will take forever. Time is entirely relative and what we make of it.

I've had a love affair with scheduling since high school. I learned to use it as a way to calm my anxiety. I felt a comfort in writing the hours down and filling them with productive activities. I filled up my time so brilliantly that there were few moments to think or be.

There is a beauty in creating a well-ordered schedule and following it. There's an even greater beauty in looking at your mental schedule, not just what your body is doing, but what your brain is doing during your days.

The real power we have over time isn't in setting aside hours for different activities. The real power we have is in realizing where we direct our mental energy and clearing out distractions. As we realize the things that suck up our time and drain our energy, we are presented with a choice: to hold onto them or clear them out. We all have the same amount of time, we just choose to direct it in different ways.

Look at where your mental energy disappears and see if there are opportunities for re-direction. For myself, I have noticed time disappearing due to a few things: social media, television, obsessive planning, worry, and guilt.

I was late to jump on the social media bandwagon and fell hopelessly head over heels once I did. I spent a whole hell of a lot of time meaninglessly streaming through pages. I wasted time, not just on the time I actually spent on planning or facebook page viewing, but on the drama and worry it created in my mind. Over the years, I've spent countless hours watching mystery re-runs and wasted endless hours planning things that didn't need planning.

Stopping the time drain doesn't necessarily mean cutting things out completely. I still use social media, but I switched from mindless scrolling to more targeted, intentional connections. I cleared out watching the news, but stay informed by talking with people or listening to NPR during times I set aside for that. This clears out unnecessary drama, worry, and fear. I love my planning, but I now usually limit it to during the day. For me planning at night turns what is normally a positive activity to a stressful, anxiety-producing one.

But I love my mystery reruns and I refuse to give them up! They are my treat and my absolute treasure. They also make folding laundry or paying bills significantly more pleasurable.

Where do you know time disappears on you? What choices can you make to change that? What time do you waste on fretting over what someone should or shouldn't have done or imagining a thing that could happen and worrying about it. Clearing our mental space is even more important than setting up a structured schedule. The practices below will support you in creating more time and joy in your schedule and life.

GREEN HEART PRACTICE:

IDEAL SCHEDULE

PRACTICE IN ABUNDANCE

Often abundance is the absolute last thing that people think of when it comes to time. For many of us, there's never enough! No matter how we juggle it or try to squeeze more things into a day, the more exhausted and stressed out we feel. Creating an ideal schedule that you can implement right now, not in some imaginary future, will allow you create a sense of abundance around time and a complete shift in how you experience time and your days.

Now I know that sounds like an over-reach and a big pie-in-the sky promise. I assure you, it's not. I'm a big planning person. I geek out over schedules. I often have loved the chance to add more things to my schedule, just for the sake of the challenge of figuring out how to "fit it all in", despite the crazed disaster this would present in my life. Some of you may find yourself in that story, and some of you might not. Regardless, putting an ideal schedule into place is not about time management, per se, and all about a different way of looking at and approaching time.

Here's what I mean by an ideal schedule. Ask yourself, what you would want to do if you had your ideal schedule? When I made this list, it included, time to read, see my mom, relax with my kids, go to the library, get a massage, and taking a yoga class.

What killed me, like a stab in the heart, was that my list was so small! In my ideal world, I only needed like an hour or two for myself each day! And I hadn't given myself that. I started crying over this realization.

My coach invited me to plan out my schedule for the next week and put all of these things first and schedule the rest of my week after, around them.

This seemed impossible.

At first.

Then I thought, well, how could I make these happen in different ways than I'd thought they had to? I wanted a massage and I'd envisioned going to a massage center which seemed overwhelming financially and scheduling wise. Could I make that happen in another way? I invited one of my friends who is a massage therapist over and she brought her table to my house. I made her dinner and gave her money. Everyone won!

I just couldn't get myself to a yoga class, despite having a free membership where I teach. The day after, I discovered a friend of mine, Liz Lockwood, had created an online meditation and yoga membership entitled "Path to Peace". Even better, the theme for the month was "Self-Love". This let me get the benefits of yoga and meditation in my own home. A bonus was that it was someone I knew and I got warm fuzzies from knowing that I was supporting her growth and abundance in her work.

Instead of hanging out at home and watching TV, I took the kids to an activity at the library. My son played chess, my daughter talked with friends, and I got to be around all those lovely books and adorable little people. (Toddlers are especially fun when you aren't responsible for them.)

I began to read each day, while taking a bath or during time I would normally watch TV or zone out on social media. I made sure to spend time more regularly with my mom, which always makes me 1,000 times happier. (She is the most adorable and loving person on the face of the earth.)

When I led with the commitment to honor my time first and

decided it was happening, everything fell into place around it. Time literally seemed to expand. I felt so much better and the rest of my life was relieved of so much struggle. Work was more enjoyable, time with my kids was more enjoyable, and I ended up getting way more done. Instead of robbing time from myself, giving myself time actually ADDED more time for everything else in my life. It felt like magic. It wasn't. It was just a decision to change.

"Love yourself first and everything else will fall in line. You really have to love yourself to get anything done in this world." - Lucille Ball

Green Heart Practice:
Time Release Meditation
A Practice in Abundance

This is my most powerful meditation. If you do nothing else in the book, please try this on. It has helped me through a myriad of catastrophic days. It has also helped me through many very normal days that, for some reason, I felt completely overwhelmed by.

This meditation is called the time release meditation for two reasons. First, you will literally release the control time has on you. Second, you will feel the results of the meditation throughout the rest of the day, just as you would a time release capsule.

Sit comfortably. If you are on the floor, sit on a rolled up blanket or bolster. You may want support for your back. This practice generally takes between 7-11 minutes, but can be stretched out for longer if you like. I developed this practice as a way of clearing out heavy energy around the past and a sense of overwhelm/confusion over the future. It is often my main meditation practice, and is especially helpful in grounding.

Take a few deep breaths. Settle into your body.

Ask "Where am I coming from?" Let the brain go where it wants. Anywhere. Let the thoughts flow. Your mind may run through what you did just before sitting down or your entire morning. It may stretch back to last week. The phone call conversation you had last week that you felt like an idiot on. Or to the time you dropped a plate in a department store when you were 11. Let whatever memory needs to play, play out. Check in with your breath. Stay for approximately 3-5 minutes. You may go to events or feelings or hippy-dippy thoughts like "I came from LOVE!" (I like those days). Once you feel complete, take 3 deep breaths.

Question 2, where am I now? Feel this moment for all it is. You may stretch your body. Focuses in on your senses and feel into the body. What is actually happening right in this moment? What are you feeling in his moment? Are you safe and at peace? In pain? Smiling? Right now. Once complete, take 3 big breaths again.

Question 3, where am I going to? Play out your day and see it going well. All the steps, meetings, interactions, calls. See yourself moving through it calmly, with confidence. Fast forward to a year or five from now and imagine everything you want in that time and space. End with three deep breaths.

You may access a recording of this meditation here: www.vimeo.com/greenheartliving

"If you are depressed, you are living in the past. If you are anxious, you are living in the future. If you are at peace, you are living in the present."

- Lao Tzo

Green Heart Practice:

Tune In & Drop Out

A Practice in Compassion

Tune in: Throughout the day, sense into your body. Are there times your shoulders lift up, your stomach feels off, your heart aches or your head spins? When does that happen? Bring a small journal or notepad with you. Any time you get these body sensations that feel like you are tightening up, your body is shielding itself from something it perceives as an assault. Jot down what is going on at the time. Who was around? Where were you? What media was on? You may do this for one day or several, whichever you are able to get a good sense from.

Drop out: Reflect on your list. What actions could you start tomorrow to reduce or eliminate things? If you consistently feel awful around certain people, give yourself permission to limit your interactions with them, or find support where you need it. When you realize that something feels heavy or toxic, take action! Drop out. Make the conscious choice to give yourself the space from situations that feel heavy or toxic. If you can't see a way to do this, talk to someone else about it. They might see something else you don't.

I eliminated watching TV news several years ago. In a world that focuses news on fear-mongering I feel significantly better off. Same with social media. There are many benefits to it, but it can become a constant habit that is very addictive. If you discover TV or social media is creating unhealthy stress or drama in your life, you may wish to direct your energy in another way.

7 COMMUNITY

"A dream you dream alone is only a dream. A dream you dream together is reality." - John Lennon

"If you want to view paradise, simply look around and view it. Anything you want to do, do it. Want to change the world? There's simply nothing to it." - Willy Wonka

Calling all community rockstars! It's time to create the world we want. What do you want the world to look like?

Rather than thinking of fighting what we DON'T want, think of what we DO want. What world do we want to create? Each day we can find ways (big and small) to move closer to it. Believe in the dream, even if it seems impossible. I have had more "impossible" things happen in my life than I can count. If people tell you it's impossible, it will be for them, but not for you. Find your people, your cheerleaders, your fellow dreamers. Find the people that want to make the world a better place and believe that it can be. Don't waste your energy on people that don't believe it. Focus your energy on creating the world you want and live in it. In Ghandi's famous words, "Be the change you wish to see." It might feel remarkably strange to live that way and other people might view you as different. That's okay.

The following pages have some practices that will support you in shining your light in your community.

Green Heart Practice:
Envision the World You Want
A Practice In Abundance

Create a Vision Board for the world you would like to live in. Include pictures from magazines that illustrate this world, words that invoke that world for you and anything specific from your own life that you'd like to include. This practice helps shift the focus from what is wrong in the world, to what kind of world we want to create. Even if it seems impossible and you have literally no idea how it would become possible, dream the biggest, most beautiful picture of the world you want. Commit to taking actions, small and big, each day to get just a little closer to your big dream. To see examples of vision boards and collages you can look at facebook.com/greenheartliving

"Why, sometimes I've believed as many as six impossible things before breakfast."
- Lewis Carroll in Alice in Wonderland

GREEN HEART PRACTICE:

BE A LEADER EVERYWHERE

A PRACTICE IN ABUNDANCE

Leadership doesn't mean you have a bunch of followers or are better than anyone else. It means showing up and deciding to make a difference in situations, rather than sitting back and letting them happen to you. It means seeing the good and the talents of others and drawing them out.

Take a day and decide to show up as leader everywhere. This means where you see something wrong or off, you will find a way to make it better. Consider yourself 100% responsible for situations and relationships. Focus on what you can do to make the situation better, including who you can inspire and empower to make a difference around you.

Whether or not others respond is all on them. How you show up and respond, is all on you. Showing up ready to make a difference is stepping into leadership everywhere.

"When the best leader's work is done the people say, 'We did it ourselves.'" - Lao Tzu

Green Heart Practice:
Metta Meditation
A Practice in Compassion

We will now revisit the Metta meditation here. Think of extending loving kindness out to include everyone, including animals, strangers, and all beings in the world. Make sure to include yourself in this.

May We Be Safe

May We Be Happy

May We Be Healthy

May We Live With Ease of Heart

And Balance

GREEN HEART PRACTICE:

FIND YOUR TRIBE

A PRACTICE IN COMPASSION

Once you've figured out your life purpose and have a clear vision of the world you want to create, shouldn't it be easy to just make it happen? Don't we wish.

The face is, you are entirely capable of rocking out your life purpose on your own. If you are anything like most of us, however, you have a lifetime of experience living a different way. It will prove challenging to dream big and take chances, in a world where we are taught to play it safe and careful. It is important to create structures of support to keep you moving towards your goals.

One important structure of support is to find your tribe. Your tribe includes people who will encourage you to let your light shine, rather than hide it; people who believe in your highest self and will take a stand for that greatness; people who want you to succeed and get nothing from cutting you down.

This past year I have experienced firsthand the benefits of a formal, intentional structure of support. The yearlong structure of the Accomplishment Coaching Life Coach and Leadership program provided a structure of support which helped me to create radical shifts in my life. It multiplied what I was capable of alone and provided options that weren't even on my radar as possible before.

There can be incredible value in choosing or creating a formal structure of support and committing to working with it for a dedicated amount of time.

Coaching Groups are excellent places to find a tribe of people that will take a stand for your goals, hold you accountable when you stop believing in yourself and take a stand for you. Groups can be local and in-person or meet through virtual meeting formats. Green Heart Living offers group coaching experiences to help you easily connect with a tribe of people that are committed to supporting each other and taking a stand for your highest self. You can find more information at www.greenheartliving.net

You may also form your own group around a common interest or need. Need support around caring for your children and yourself too? Form a babysitting co-operative where parents create a network of support to swap childcare. See a problem in the community you want to solve? Use social media to gather a group of people to create change. Want to make the world a greener and more sustainable place? Form a book club to read texts like "No Impact Man" or "Animal, Vegetable, Miracle" and create actions around these together. Want to bring more art or writing into the world? Create a writing group or painting club with people in your town.

"Plenty of people will think you're crazy, no matter what you do. Don't let that stop you from finding the people who think you're incredible - the ones who need to hear your voice, because it reminds them of their own. Your tribe. They're out there. Don't let your critics interfere with your search for them." - Vironika Tugaleva

Green Heart Practice:
Put on Your Green Glasses
A Practice in Gratitude

We live in an increasingly bizarre world, so bringing in a reference to Wizard of Oz seems exquisitely appropriate. Visitors to Oz were given green glasses, making the world dazzling, shiny, and green. I will invite you to put on your green glasses, seeing the world in a different way than you might be used to looking at it.

It is very easy to look at the world and see what's wrong. To see the heartbreak, the hunger, the corruption, the violence. The media, especially that in the states, encourages this lens. What makes news? The ugly, the shocking, the things you can't look away from.

I invite you to re-shift your focus from one of complaint and seeing the broken, to one of gratitude and seeing what's working. Clear out media streams that fill your head with the former. This doesn't mean ignoring what's wrong, but it means focusing on what's RIGHT. When we focus on what's working and find ways to contribute our energy towards that, you will find a completely different experience in life. Rather than focusing your energy on fighting what's not working, focus on creating the solutions. There will always be fights to be had, and things to change, and those fights can be valuable and important. By focusing, however, on contributing to solutions (both in our own lives and for lives the globe over) we not only feel better about our daily experience with life, we also can make a grander difference and bring more light and love to the community.

"Your attitude is like a box of crayons that color your world. Constantly color your picture gray, and your picture will always be bleak. Try adding some bright colors to the picture by including humor, and your picture begins to lighten up." - Allen Klein

GREEN HEART PRACTICE:
GREEN HEART, GREEN WORLD MEDITATION
A PRACTICE IN COMPASSION

Lay down and get comfortable. As you breath in, imagine the breath bringing nourishing energy into every cell in your body. Each breath in flows to exactly where your body and heart need healing. Take a few minutes to breath into this space of healing, nourishment, and peace.

Once you have developed a sense of this loving, healing energy within your body, begin imagining that you can share the energy with each breath out. Extend that healing energy to everyone in the room, in the building, on your street, in your town, in your country, in your world. With each breath, extend your reach further and further out.

"If in our daily life, we can smile, if we can be peaceful and happy, not only we, but everyone will profit from it. This is the most basic kind of peace work." - Thich Nhat Hanh

Green Heart Practice:

11 Steps to A Healthier & Happier Community

A Practice in Compassion

1. **SMILE** at people.

2. **SLOW DOWN** and breathe.

3. **TURN OFF** your electronics and look around you.

4. **GET TOGETHER** with people that are different from you - different ages, genders, religion, sexual orientations, political leanings, etc...

5. **GET CURIOUS.** Ask people what THEY want to see in the community. Ask big questions. Everyone has something inside them we can learn from.

6. **VOLUNTEER.** Find out what opportunities exist in your community by connecting with nonprofits, including your local United Way.

7. **START SOMETHING.** A book club, a supper club, a community garden, a recycling program. Create some way to connect with your neighbors in a new way.

8. **LEARN** what's already going on in your community and see if there's a way you can help support it.

9. **PLANT SEEDS** for something bigger than yourself.

10. **THANK PEOPLE** at every opportunity.

11. **LEAD.** Show up as someone who will take action and make a difference. Show up as leader. Everywhere.

"Making a dream into reality begins with what you have not with what you are waiting on." - T. F. Hodge

8 LET YOUR LIGHT SHINE

"Believe, not in my ability to bring about change, but in yours."
- President Barack Obama

"Do you like real life? My favorite thing is real life."
- James Bohmier, Age 6

Do the world a favor and find your big, beautiful dream and take action towards it each day. Find your dharma and let it guide you each day. Don't hide your light under a bushel. Don't let others tell you you are too bright or too much. Find your light and share that good with the world. If others can't handle it, it is their loss. Don't let it be yours. Or the world's.

You have one very precious, real life and you get to choose what to do with it! By contributing each day to the light in the world, you add a beautiful abundance to the world. Your abundant light illuminates and eliminates the darkness. By finding more ways you to contribute your light, you add to the collective compassion on the earth.

In his final formal address as President, President Obama said, "Believe, not in my ability to bring about change...but in yours." I heard this and immediately wept, for a multitude of reasons. Often, we look towards others to shine their light so we can follow.

Let us follow Obama's words of wisdom. We all have a light to shine on the world. Imagine what the world could be if we all shined bright and gave others the courage to do the same.

ABOUT THE AUTHOR

Elizabeth Hill has more than a decade of experience helping nonprofits create measurable change in their communities. Elizabeth is the founder of Green Heart Living, a mindful approach to living focusing on gratitude, abundance and compassion. She works with nonprofits and community leaders to make the world a better place for all. Trained as a yoga teacher, social worker and life coach, she often weaves creativity, spirituality and mindfulness into her work with clients. Elizabeth lives in Avon, CT with her family and the neighborhood bears. You can learn more about her and her work at www.greenheartliving.net